HOW TO WORK WITH
ANGELS

HOW TO WORK WITH
ANGELS

ELIZABETH CLARE PROPHET

SUMMIT UNIVERSITY PRESS®

HOW TO WORK WITH ANGELS
by Elizabeth Clare Prophet
Copyright © 1998 by Summit University Press
All rights reserved

Library of Congress Control Number: 2002106126
ISBN: 0-922729-41-7
SUMMIT UNIVERSITY ❂ PRESS

Printed in the United States of America.
08 07 06 05 04   9 8 7 6 5

CONTENTS

MY RELATIONSHIP WITH ANGELS   1

How to Work with Angels:
A TEN-STEP PLAN   5

    1. Make room in your life for angels   11

    2. Pray aloud   13

    3. Use the name of God   15

    4. Give your prayers and decrees daily   17

    5. Ask for help   19

    6. Repeat decrees and prayers   21

    7. Send your prayer to the right address   23

    8. Be specific   25

    9. Visualize what you want to happen   29

    10. Expect to be surprised   31

    A Call Is Answered   34

ANGELS OF PROTECTION   39

    Archangel Michael to the Rescue   43

CONTENTS

ANGELS OF ILLUMINATION   47

    Passing the Test   51

ANGELS OF LOVE   53

    The Finding Angels   58

ANGELS OF GUIDANCE   61

    Visiting the Angels at Home   65

ANGELS OF HEALING   69

    Mary Points the Way   74

    Healing Blessings from the
    Queen of Angels   76

ANGELS OF PEACE   79

    Archangel Uriel's Exercise
    for Letting Go   84

ANGELS OF JOY   87

DECREES AND PRAYERS TO THE ANGELS   93

PICTURE CREDITS   112

MY RELATIONSHIP
WITH ANGELS

While water-skiing on the Navesink River in New Jersey when I was eighteen, I had one of my early experiences with angels. It was a beautiful day and I was headed out toward the ocean. Suddenly I realized that I had entered another dimension. I could see not thousands but millions of angels.

I saw that they were my friends, brothers and sisters, spiritual companions. I also realized that I had a calling from God and that I would be shown what to do in order to fulfill it. And I knew that I would never be alone because the angels would always be with me.

That vision stayed with me through my college years as I searched for greater contact with the angels and other beings of light. In 1961 I met Mark Prophet, who would become both my teacher and my husband. Mark was able to receive inspired revelations from the angels and from other spiritual beings known as Ascended Masters. I realized it was also my calling to receive these revelations, which are called dictations.

Mark passed on in 1973 and I have continued his work through The Summit Lighthouse, the spiritual organization he founded. Between us, we have taken thousands of dictations, which are the source of the angel quotations and many of the prayers in this book.

During years of communing with the

angels, I have developed a personal relationship with them. They are always near—they whisper words of warning, guidance and encouragement. I know that Archangel Michael and his blue-flame angels have saved me and my family from serious harm dozens of times. And my angel secretaries even help me to organize my days.

In the following pages you will learn how you can develop your own relationship with the angels or expand the contact that you already have with them. The angels want to be a part of your life. They are ready to help you solve problems, big and small, and bring you closer to your Higher Self—your real, or spiritual, self.

Just follow the steps outlined here and the angels will take charge. You may not see them as they fly thick and fast about your business, but you will see the results as they respond—sometimes faster than you can ask for help!

Elizabeth Clare Prophet

NOTE: All the stories in this book are real. Some names, however, have been changed at the individuals' request.

HOW TO WORK WITH ANGELS:
A TEN-STEP PLAN

*E*veryone has heard angel stories. Angels pull people back from the edges of cliffs and out of the paths of oncoming trains. They warn people to avoid dangerous situations. They guide those facing tough decisions. They comfort, enlighten and heal.

But how can you get the angels to help you? You are about to learn how to develop a relationship with the angels so that when you call, they answer. You'll read how people have used specific techniques to receive angelic guidance and inspiration. And how the angels go to work for them, handling everything from the mundane details of life to miracle cures to highway rescue.

Take Alex, who lost control of his car on an icy road. As he slid toward a precipice, he called to Archangel Michael. His car immediately moved back into the middle of the road—"almost as if it had been pushed by hand." Then there was Verlene, who got angelic assistance when she went blank while taking a test.

The first thing to consider is: What are angels and why do they answer our prayers?

Angels are to God what sunbeams are to the sun. God created the angels to serve and minister to us. Answering our prayers is their reason for being. Although we live in the material world, we have a special link to God through his angels. And we each have a part of God, a divine spark, within us that allows us to ask the angels for help—and to expect results!

As long as what you are asking them to do is positive and will not hurt others or interfere with your life plan, the angels will answer your call. Not only can you ask them to help you personally but you can also direct them—even command them—to perform larger tasks, like stopping crime and saving children from violence and drugs.

The angels are literally waiting for you to give them assignments. For there is one rule they seldom break. They don't intervene in our world unless we ask them to. Keep that in mind as you study this ten-point plan for getting the angels to work for you.

 *For he shall give his angels charge over thee, to keep thee in all thy ways.*

Psalm 91:11

❧ 1 ❧

Make room in your life for angels

The angels live in the world of Spirit, the heaven-world, and we live in the world of matter. Angels naturally gravitate toward their home. So if you want the angels to feel comfortable with you, you need to make your world—your thoughts, feelings and surroundings—more like theirs. To paraphrase the Epistle of James: Draw near to the angels and they will draw near to you.

The angels are comfortable with thoughts of peace and love, not with irritation and aggression. You may not be able to put out of your mind the rude driver who cut in front of you on your way home. But you can free yourself from the irritation, starting by communing with the angels for just a few minutes a day.

First, separate yourself from distractions. Turn off the radio and TV, go into a room by yourself or to your favorite nature spot, imagine an angel in your mind (it helps to have a picture of your favorite angel nearby) and commune with the angels.

Simply talk to the angels about your problems. Talk as if you were talking to your best friend. And then listen. Be silent and wait for the thoughts that the angels will put into your mind. You may want to use some of the techniques in this book to increase the flow of positive energy from the angels.

Before long, your relationship with the angels will turn into an upward spiral: the angels will help you to feel more positive. And feeling positive will bring you closer to the angels.

Pray aloud

The angels have answered many an unspoken prayer or intense wish of the heart. You don't *have* to speak in order to get their attention, especially if you're in a place where it would be awkward, like a business meeting or on the subway. But you will get a more powerful response when you speak to them out loud.

There is power in your voice: the power to create or to destroy. God used this power when he said, "Let there be light." By using your gift of speech, you can create changes in your life.

Spoken prayer comes in different forms: songs and hymns, which have traditionally been used to summon the angels; structured prayer, like the Our Father; and unstructured prayer, in which you speak the deepest longings of your soul. You can combine all of these with "decrees" and "fiats," the new prayer forms you will learn about in this book.

Decrees allow man and God to work together for constructive change. They are spoken prayers that enable you to direct God's energy into the world. Fiats are short, powerful affirmations like "Archangel Michael, Help me! Help me! Help me!" which are effective in summoning angelic help.

Speak your decrees and fiats out loud in a strong, firm voice. Speak them at home before your altar, on the way to the bus stop, in the car, in the mountains and, most especially, in an emergency. And see how the floodgates of heaven will open for you!

Use the name of God

God is inside of you. And when you use the energy of God that is in you to direct the angels, they can answer you with all of the power of the universe.

When God spoke to Moses out of the burning bush, he revealed both his name—I AM THAT I AM—and the true nature of man. You are the bush and the fire is your divine spark, God's fire that he gives to you as his son or daughter. It is the power to create in God's name—and to command the angels.

Jesus used God's name when he said "I AM the resurrection and the life." Every time you say "I AM...," you are really saying "God in me is..." and thus drawing to

15

yourself whatever follows. When you say "I AM illumination," you are saying that God in you is attracting to you more of the quality of illumination that you already possess. Many of the decrees and fiats in this booklet use the name of God, I AM THAT I AM. Try it—and experience the increased power of your prayers.

❧ 4 ❧

Give your prayers and decrees daily

The angels are always there. But we don't always know how to reach them. The best way to make sure that the angels answer when you call them is to create a well-traveled pathway from your heart to theirs by communing with them every day. And the best way to commune with them is to schedule a daily session of prayers and devotions. It doesn't have to be long—five minutes is a great start.

Michael, a mechanic, says the angels help him all the time and that giving daily decrees helps him to stay on the same wavelength as the angels. "On my end, I'm attuned to them more," he says. When he decrees every day, he knows the angels will answer right away each time he asks for help. He says they usually show him where to find missing parts within fifteen seconds and regularly help diagnose car problems.

When you pray daily, you not only help yourself but you also help people you don't even know. The angels are looking for people who regularly invoke God's light to be their partners in planetary healing. When they find these partners, they direct light through them to help those in danger from disease, violent crime or natural disaster. Thus your daily prayers can truly make a world of difference.

❧ 5 ❧

Ask for help

Even after you have established your relationship with the angels, you still need to remember to ask for help at the time you need it. The angels respect your free will. On rare occasions, they will intercede without your speaking up. But most often, they politely wait to be called.

Michael (the mechanic) says that he sometimes struggles over a problem for a long time before he finally remembers to call for help. It often happens when he is trying to screw in a bolt in a place he can't see. "I can spend fifteen minutes trying and then I'll say, 'Angels, please help me do this,' and boom! the thing starts," he says.

❧ 6 ❧

Repeat decrees and prayers

Prayers and decrees are more powerful when you repeat them. Many Protestants avoid saying prayers more than once, seeing it as the vain repetition that Jesus advised against (Matt. 6:7). "After all," they say, "why should I have to ask God for something more than one time?" However, the Catholic and the Eastern Orthodox Churches practice repetition of the Our Father, Hail Mary and other prayers. Jewish mystics repeated the names of God. For some mystics, repetition truly becomes prayer "without ceasing" (I Thess. 5:17).

The reason it is more effective to repeat a prayer is that each time you say it, you are giving more light-energy to God and the angels. The angels can use that energy as a seed, adding more light-energy as they go about answering your request. So choose a group of prayers and decrees. Then give them every day until the angels respond.

❦ 7 ❦

Send your prayer to the right address

If you want your pipes fixed, you call a plumber. If you want to be rescued from a mugger, you call to the angels of protection. If you want a relationship fixed, you call to the angels of love.

Angels have different jobs. And they use energies of different frequencies (corresponding to different colors) to accomplish those jobs. In the following pages you will meet seven kinds of angels, along with the seven archangels who supervise them. You will also learn which angels to call to for which tasks.

The idea of seven archangels isn't new. Neither is the association of angels with colors or with spiritual fire. As early as the third century B.C., Jews wrote about seven archangels. And they believed that the angels were surrounded by spiritual flames and appeared in a variety of colors.

You can become more closely connected with the angels when you call to the archangel whose angels specialize in handling what you want done.

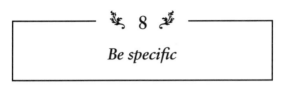

8

Be specific

Angels answer your calls with precision, and they take pride in doing so. The more specific the request, the more specific the answer will be. As long as you are living your life in harmony with the universal Source and devoting your energy to helping others, the angelic hosts will help you with the smallest details of your life.

One inspiring example is the penniless woman who turned over to God a grocery list during World War II. She asked God specifically for the exact items she needed for her family's weekend meals. Within a few hours, a man knocked on her door carrying a basket with everything she had asked for, right down to the veal, potatoes and pastry flour.

Here is how another woman worked with the angels to draw to herself the kind of truck she wanted. Danette was looking for a used Toyota 4Runner but knew that she couldn't afford the steep prices they were selling for. So she decided to leave it to the angels.

She wrote down the year, make, color, engine size, price range, mileage and type of rims and tires she wanted. She also listed that she wanted a mechanically sound car with power steering, power brakes, power windows, power locks, air conditioning and cruise control. She cut out a picture of the kind of truck she was looking for and carried it around in her wallet. Every day, she gave decrees and fiats to the angels for fifteen to forty-five minutes while looking at her list and picture.

After weeks of scanning the classifieds, Danette was a little concerned but didn't give up. "I knew the angels were working on it. . . . I wouldn't settle for less," she said. Finally, she decided to continue her search in another city, twelve hours away. Her friends there had told her that a 4Runner in her price range just wasn't to be found.

But when she looked in the paper, there it was—"a 1990 Toyota 4Runner for $3,000 less than any other I had seen!" she said. The owner had just placed the ad that day and the car fit every one of her specifications, right down to the cruise control. Her bank approved the loan and she drove home in her new 4Runner—thanking the angels all the way.

The more detailed your requests, the more satisfied you will be with the results.

Visualize what you want to happen

You can increase the power of your prayer by maintaining a strong mental picture of what you want to have happen. In addition, visualize brilliant light surrounding the problem or situation. Sometimes concentrating on a picture, as Danette did, can help too. Here is another example of how visualization works.

A group of students were driving home after attending a spiritual seminar when their car began to overheat. Since none of them had any extra money to spend on car repairs, they decided to ask the angels for help.

"Each time the needle started creeping up hotter and hotter, I would make fiery calls to the angels," said Kevin, the driver. "I told the people in the car to hold the visualization of snow, of crystal clear, cold mountain streams and ice all around the whole engine. Then we would watch the needle immediately go right back down as the temperature dropped to normal."

The group made it home safely, thanks to the angels—and an effective visualization technique! Of course, it is better to combine angelic assistance with professional help when possible.

❧ 10 ❧

Expect to be surprised

The question occurs to just about anyone who has ever thought about angels: Why do the angels answer some prayers and not others?

Why does one person pray for ten years without getting what he wants while another gets it immediately? Why are some houses destroyed by fire or flood while others are left untouched? Surely the angels hear everyone's prayers.

One reason is that the angels' ability to respond to our prayers is based upon the cumulative effects of our past actions—our good and bad deeds from this and previous lifetimes, also known as karma. The angels are neither genies nor Santa Claus. They must play by the rules of karma. When we pray and give devotion to the angels, they can sometimes eliminate the effects of karma, but often they can only reduce them.

The angels hear all of your prayers. But in order for your requests to be granted, they must fulfill three conditions: (1) they may not interfere with God's plan for your soul (or with your karma); (2) they must not be harmful to you or anyone else; (3) the timing must be right.

You could pray for years to win the lottery and not win. But you might get something you didn't expect, like a higher-paying job that leads you in new directions. Perhaps the angels couldn't answer your prayer to win the lottery because your soul needs to learn the lesson of earning a living. But they did answer in the way that was best for you.

If you follow the steps in this booklet and still find that you don't get an answer, the angels may be trying to tell you something. It might be time to revise your prayer and try again. Keep praying, and know that the angels will give you the best answer that they can based on your soul's needs. (See "A Call Is Answered" on page 34.) Prayer always bears fruit. You just have to know where to look.

A CALL IS ANSWERED

When she was sixteen, Lucy Krasowski had a premonition that she would die a violent death at age thirty. The feeling didn't go away with adolescence. At twenty-five, she began asking God to keep her from the death she felt was fated.

In the meantime, she had become a Montreal police officer. Although violence against police officers is rarer in Canada than in America, Lucy felt that she was in danger and asked God to lead her to prayers for protection. She had heard that Archangel Michael was the patron of police officers and so she was looking for prayers to him.

She was thirty when she first attended a Summit Lighthouse Study Group meeting. There she learned decrees and prayers to Archangel Michael as well as the fiat "Archangel Michael, Help me! Help me! Help me!" She quickly memorized the decrees and began giving them on her way to and from work and during breaks. "I was in almost constant communion [with the angels]," she recalled.

On May 22, 1993, Lucy gave two hours of decrees to Archangel Michael before going to work at 8 p.m. That night, she and her partner were searching for an assault suspect. They pulled up to a man and asked him if he had seen anything. He leveled a 9 mm pistol at them and demanded their weapons. When they hesitated, he shot them both—Lucy in the head, face and leg and her partner in the head.

Lucy opened her door and fell out, trying to take cover under the car. "Lord Michael! Help me! Help me! Help me!" she called aloud. Her call frightened the gunman, who ran away, thinking she was radioing for help. This gave her the time to actually get to the radio. (The gunman was later caught and convicted.)

Although Lucy had been seriously wounded, the bullets missed her spinal cord and major blood vessels. "She... was probably within millimeters of having something tragic happen," said her surgeon, Dr. Philip Dahan.

She attributes the near misses as well as her swift recovery to Archangel Michael. She never went into shock and was walking around two days after the shooting. Ten days after that, she left the hospital. Although her hearing was impaired and some of her facial muscles were paralyzed, today she is hearing in the low normal range. Lucy calls her recovery "awesome," especially since the doctors originally told her that she would never again hear out of her right ear.

Why didn't Archangel Michael keep her from being shot in the first place? She believes that her karma—the cumulative effect of her past actions—prevented him from stopping the bullets. But she thinks her prayers enabled him to redirect them so that she was not killed. Although her karma may have destined her to die at age thirty, her determination to live and her choice to pray changed her "fate."

"My karma didn't allow the bullets to be stopped, but what Archangel Michael did was just as good. He saved my life," she said. "God doesn't always answer our prayers the way we expect him to."

ANGELS OF PROTECTION

COLOR: Blue

ARCHANGEL: Michael, "Who is like God"

SPIRITUAL HOME:
Banff, near Lake Louise, Canada

ASK THEM FOR:
- *Spiritual Gifts:* freedom from fear and self-doubt, strengthening of your faith, perfecting of your soul.
- *Practical Assistance:* protection from physical and spiritual dangers—everything from traffic accidents and burglaries to psychic aggression; exorcism of demons.
- *World Service:* inspiration for leaders, improvement of government.

*J*ewish, Christian and Islamic scriptures all revere Archangel Michael. Jewish mystical tradition identifies him as the Captain of the LORD's Host, who appeared to Joshua before the battle of Jericho, and also as the angel who guided Israel through the wilderness and saved the three Hebrew boys from Nebuchadnezzar's fiery furnace.

Archangel Michael and his angels of protection can answer your SOS calls best when you pray to them daily. Thousands of people have experienced miracles that they believe were made possible by their strong relationship with the blue-flame angels.

People like Daniel. He's an airline pilot who had begun decreeing to the angels of protection for about twenty minutes a day. One day he took his two young sons out for a tractor ride near their home outside Dallas when a tree branch fell on his neck and back. With his back covered in blood, he was somehow able to drive the quarter mile back to his house. He didn't remember the drive, but four-year-old Christopher did: "Daddy drove the tractor home, but a big blue angel came down and sat on the front of the tractor," he said. The angel told him that his daddy would be all right.

Daniel recovered quickly without surgery, although the hospital staff told him he was lucky not to be a quadriplegic. He believes his decrees enabled the angel to save him. (See pages 93–111 for prayers and decrees, to the angels.)

ARCHANGEL MICHAEL
TO THE RESCUE

Kelly and her friends Wayne, Russell and Heather had been decreeing to the angels for only a few weeks when they needed emergency help. The four teenagers piled into Wayne's compact sedan and gave Archangel Michael's "Traveling Protection" decree before heading off for a church picnic.

Just after they exited the highway and were on an overpass, a fully loaded 18-wheeler ran a red light and plowed into their car. The truck dragged the car under its wheels for 500 feet before stopping.

Kelly was in the backseat on the passenger's side—the side where the truck impacted. She was pinned in the crushed metal from the bottom of her feet to the middle of her chest. One wheel of the stalled truck was directly above her body and she couldn't breathe.

"Do your calls!" yelled Heather, who was also in the backseat. Kelly couldn't speak, but she made a silent prayer to Archangel Michael.

Strange as it sounds, Kelly swears the truck instantly lifted a few inches, giving her time to twist the upper part of her body free. Then the weight of the truck descended again. "All of a sudden I could breathe," said Kelly. Her first words aloud were, "Thank you, Archangel Michael!"

During the nearly two hours it took to get her out of the wreckage, she said she remained "perfectly calm," comforted by the presence of Michael and his angels.

After three surgeries, she still has some hip problems but says it's "nothing you couldn't live with." Wayne was uninjured, while Russell received a blow to his head and Heather a broken arm. Kelly says she knows that Archangel Michael saved them all from death or lasting injury.

—FIAT—

ARCHANGEL MICHAEL,
HELP ME! HELP ME! HELP ME!

ANGELS OF ILLUMINATION

COLOR: Yellow

ARCHANGEL: Jophiel, "Beauty of God"

SPIRITUAL HOME: Near Lanchow, north central China

ASK THEM FOR:

• *Spiritual gifts:* wisdom, illumination, understanding, inspiration, knowledge, clear seeing, connection with your Higher Self.

• *Practical assistance:* help in absorbing information, studying for and passing tests; freedom from addictions; dissolution of ignorance, pride and narrow-mindedness.

• *World service:* exposure of wrongdoing in government and corporations, help in fighting pollution and cleaning up our planet.

We've all seen it in cartoons: Pop! the light bulb goes on over someone's head. "I have an idea!" they say. Even Einstein had a sudden flash of insight that inspired his theory of relativity. But where does the inspiration come from?

Many of our ideas actually come from Archangel Jophiel and the angels of illumination, who put us in touch with the mind of God, the source of all creativity. These angels bring us our great inspirations and life-changing revelations. They help us to contact our Higher Self and even to absorb information and pick up new skills. Their primary purpose is to rescue us from ignorance, which can be defined as blindness to our oneness with God.

When you commune with these angels,

they will free you from anything that blocks your oneness with your Higher Self, including self-doubt, fear, lack of self-esteem, and addictions of all kinds—from chocolate to nicotine. They can even help you to increase your mental capacity and use a greater percentage of your brain.

So talk to them about questions on your mind and the best way to approach a problem. Ask them to inspire you with the words for your poem, the plot for your novel, the arguments for your brief. You can rely on them to do all this, as well as keep you in touch with your Higher Self, when you daily invoke the flame of illumination.

PASSING THE TEST

Has it happened to you? You study hard for a test and then when it's sitting in front of you on an empty desk and the clock is ticking, you can't remember a thing you studied.

Verlene had always had a hard time taking exams. Even if she had studied hard, she would go blank when faced with a test. When she was studying to become a Realtor in Illinois, she did so well in the class exercises that her instructor told her, "You'll ace this exam."

"No, I won't," she thought with a sinking feeling, "because I never do." Sure enough, when she got to the exam room and opened up her test, her mind went blank.

She made a silent prayer to the angels to illumine her mind. Suddenly the answers began flowing into her head, her pen moved across the page and she was able to take the test.

She didn't find out her score, since the scores aren't released, but she did pass. She believes the angels helped her make it through. She says that once she got going on the test, "I enjoyed it. It was kind of a breeze."

—FIAT—

ANGELS BRIGHT FROM STARRY HEIGHT, CHARGE MY BEING AND MIND WITH LIGHT!

ANGELS OF LOVE

COLOR: Pink

ARCHANGEL: Chamuel, "He who sees God"

SPIRITUAL HOME: St. Louis, Missouri

ASK THEM FOR:

- *Spiritual gifts:* love, compassion, mercy, creativity, forgiveness; dissolution of feelings of selfishness, self-dislike, self-condemnation and low self-esteem; preparation to receive the Holy Spirit.

- *Practical assistance:* protection against malice, slander and misunderstanding; inauguration of new friendships and relationships; repairing of damaged relationships; help in getting along with others; help in finding a job; locating lost objects .

- *World service:* healing of ethnic and racial tension.

$\mathcal{L}$ove can be both gentle and fierce, and so can Archangel Chamuel and his angels. They may appear surrounded by layers of gossamer light to comfort a frightened child. Or they may put on their armour to fight the forces of cruelty and hatred that cause many of the problems in families and relationships.

The angels of love help you fight the forces of anti-love, which bring about addictions and psychological problems such as depression and compulsive behavior. When you feel yourself in the grips of desire for nicotine, when your self-esteem is low or when you feel powerless against forces of racial division and tension in your neighborhood, give the powerful fiat to Chamuel and the angels of love (p. 57). Repeat the second part, "Be gone, forces of anti-love!"

nine times or more.

The angels of love also specialize in making your life run more smoothly. Archangel Chamuel will assign angels to help you in your daily life as if they were your personal staff. You can ask them to run errands, prepare the way for successful meetings and undertake special projects on behalf of your family, your business or your church.

They are experts at improving communication between people. You can ask them to help those in your household understand each other and to help you to be a better listener to meet others' needs.

So if your children are fighting or you aren't getting along with your spouse, boss or neighbors, or if you don't seem to be able to attract the kind of relationships you want, try adding some prayers to the angels of love

to your daily ritual. See how they will trans-
form you and those who are closest to you.

—FIAT—

IN THE NAME OF GOD,
I AM THAT I AM, IN THE NAME
OF ARCHANGEL CHAMUEL:
BE GONE, FORCES OF ANTI-LOVE!

THE
FINDING ANGELS

Angels of every sort help us find lost objects. But the angels of love are especially concerned with providing for our comfort and well-being.

They can find things like lost jewelry, clothing, even misplaced documents. It works like this. You make the call: "Angels, please help me find my _____ ." Suddenly you remember where it is, get a vision of its location or even find it in a place where you have already looked.

Patricia lost an earring in a busy mall. Her friend Carol told her to call to the finding angels. Although skeptical, she followed her friend's advice. Suddenly her eyes landed on the spot under a counter where the earring had rolled.

Alice, a nurse, regularly asks the angels to help her find missing objects in the hospital. She can often find things like special syringes or tubing that no one else can locate. "It's almost like the angels show me in my inner vision where I should go to look for it," she says.

 We will do anything you ask, as long as it is lawful for us to do in the sight of God.

Archangel Chamuel

ANGELS OF GUIDANCE

COLOR: White

ARCHANGEL: Gabriel, "God is my strength"

SPIRITUAL HOME: Between Sacramento
and Mount Shasta, California

ASK THEM FOR:

- *Spiritual gifts:* guidance in creating your
spiritual life; revelation of your life plan and
purpose; dissolution of discouragement; joy,
happiness and fulfillment.

- *Practical assistance:* help in establishing dis-
cipline and order in your life: the organization
of your emotional, mental and physical environment, including such things as home purchases
and new directions in your education and career.

- *World service:* help in organizing peace-
keeping operations, distribution of food and
medical assistance, relief for victims of natural
disasters.

*G*abriel and the angels of guidance will help you to understand and perform your life's calling. In the Book of Daniel, Gabriel helps the prophet to interpret his visions and gives him wisdom and understanding. In Luke, Gabriel tells Mary that she will be the mother of the Son of God. Muslims believe that Gabriel instructed the prophets and dictated the Koran to Muhammad.

Gabriel and his angels will help you to understand the plan that you, your Higher Self and a board of spiritual beings worked out for your life before you were born. They will help you to remember what you need to do to fulfill that plan and to meet the people who can help you carry it out.

These angels will also help you to defend your life plan against whatever opposes it—

things like discouragement, ridicule and lack of money and resources. They will help you to organize your life so that you are able to fulfill your daily obligations while working toward your larger goals.

The angels of guidance will speak to you when you make a point of listening to them. One of the best techniques for summoning angelic guidance is to ask the angels to transfer information to your mind while you sleep. In fact, they may already be doing this.

Have you ever awakened with a wonderful, positive feeling and a sense of direction? If you have, it's a good bet that your soul has been in the angels' spiritual homes while your body was asleep. Use the following technique to increase your nightly contact. And then hold on to those happy thoughts as you make your life happen with the angels of guidance!

The archangels keep spiritual homes, or retreats, in the heaven-world over certain powerful spots in the earth. Each retreat is a gathering point for angels and an instruction center for our souls while we sleep at night.

You can visit universities of the Spirit, which have libraries and lecture halls where you can learn about almost any subject you can imagine—from personal psychology to getting along with other people to understanding math concepts. Your conscious mind won't necessarily remember everything you have learned at these universities of the Spirit, but the information may come to you as inspiration and flashes of insight.

Select the retreat that you want to visit based on the kind of spiritual work you are doing. Here is an example of a prayer you can give before going to sleep. Insert the name and retreat location of the archangel you want to visit.

In the name of my own Real Self, I call to the angels to take me in my soul consciousness to the etheric retreat of _____

[Archangel Gabriel and the angels of guidance,] *located*

[between Sacramento and Mount Shasta, California].

I ask that I be filled and inspired with the will of God. And I ask _____

[Archangel Gabriel and the angels of guidance]

to _____ [insert request]

_____.

I ask that all information necessary for the fulfillment of my divine plan be released

to my outer waking consciousness as it is re-
quired. I thank you and I accept it done this
hour in full power.

I am here and I shall not leave
you . . . until you have fulfilled your
reason for being.

Archangel Gabriel

ANGELS OF HEALING

COLOR: Green

ARCHANGEL: Raphael, "God has healed"

SPIRITUAL HOME: Fátima, Portugal

ASK THEM FOR:

- *Spiritual gifts:* wholeness, vision, spiritual sight, inspiration of truth.
- *Practical assistance:* healing of body, mind, soul and spirit; inspiration for the study and practice of music, mathematics, science and both traditional and alternative medicine; meeting of physical needs such as food, clothing, shelter, tools of your trade.
- *World service:* repairing of rifts between nations, healing of those injured on the battlefield, inspiration for new cures for diseases.

*R*aphael is known as the angel of science, knowledge and healing. One Jewish text says he revealed to Noah the curative power of plants; another tells how he healed a blind man and bound a demon. Catholics revere him as the angel who healed the sick at the pool of Bethesda. The Book of Enoch tells us that his responsibilities include healing the diseases and wounds of men. Raphael works with the healing angels and Mary, Queen of Angels, to heal diseases of body, mind and soul.

When approaching a physical or mental health problem, first get help from the appropriate professional, whether a medical doctor, chiropractor or mental health practitioner, and then set the angels to work. Ask them to remove any negative energy that is causing the condition. Then ask them to overshadow and work through the professionals you have chosen.

All the while, pray daily to the angels for healing, visualizing God's healing light in a brilliant emerald color surrounding and infusing the injured or diseased area. Always call to the angels of protection to work with the angels of healing. Often the healing process needs to be protected from invasive forces—everything from infection to negative energy.

If you pray and don't see immediate results, don't give up. Raphael has explained that physical healing is not always possible. Your karma may require that you experience physical pain or disease for a period of time. However, your prayers may work to heal the diseases of soul and spirit that led you to make the initial karma.

Always be prepared for miraculous results. You never know when your prayer or an act of grace may allow the karma to be set aside and you will see the beautiful work of the healing angels as they restore broken souls and bodies.

We come for the healing of the soul, the mind and the heart, knowing that all else will follow as the healing of the body.

Archangel Raphael

MARY POINTS THE WAY

Margaret knew that breast cancer was a leading cause of death for women her age, and so she was doing all the right things. She gave herself regular exams and went for her scheduled checkups. But she might not have noticed a lump until it was too late if she hadn't gotten help from a higher source.

She had been praying and singing hymns daily to the Blessed Mother for about three weeks when she received tangible proof of her presence. "I woke in the middle of the night after a dream of a beautiful, illumined hand coming down through clouds, indicating a previously unnoticed lump under my left breast, on the rib," she said. "My fingers were directly on it." The surgeon found that there was indeed a lump, which he quickly removed. Although the tissue was not malignant, it contained some abnormal cells that could have turned cancerous if it had not been removed.

Margaret's devotions included the New Age rosary and songs and hymns to the Blessed Mother from the album *Sanctissima*. She believes it was the power of her prayers that allowed Mother Mary to bring the lump to her attention.

—FIAT—

I AM THE RESURRECTION AND THE
LIFE OF MY PERFECT HEALTH
NOW MADE MANIFEST!

Mary, the mother of Jesus, is known as the Queen of Angels. She has been associated with thousands of miraculous healings, especially at Lourdes in France, Medjugorje in Bosnia and Herzegovina, and other sites where she has appeared. Many students of the Ascended Masters have reported healings that resulted from their prayers to Mother Mary given along with the Scriptural Rosary for the New Age, which Mother Mary released to me in 1972.

The rosary includes the Our Father and a revised Hail Mary that refers to us as "sons and daughters of God" rather than as "sinners." In a dictation given through me, Mary explained that the Hail Mary is meant to revere not only the mother of Jesus but also God as Mother. Thus anyone who gives the Hail Mary is accessing the energy and power of God as Mother. Mary told us that millions of angels answer when you give the Hail Mary.

Give it three times or more following your heartfelt prayers for healing or for whatever spiritual or physical gifts you require.

Hail, Mary, full of grace.
The Lord is with thee.
Blessed art thou among women
And blessed is the fruit of thy womb, Jesus.
Holy Mary, Mother of God,
Pray for us, sons and daughters of God,
Now and at the hour of our victory
Over sin, disease and death.

ANGELS OF PEACE

COLOR: Purple and gold flecked with ruby

ARCHANGEL: Uriel, "Fire of God"

SPIRITUAL HOME: Tatra Mountains,
   south of Cracow, Poland

ASK THEM FOR:

• *Spiritual gifts:* inner peace, tranquility of spirit,
untangling of knots of anger and fear in your
psyche, renewal of hope.

• *Practical assistance:* peaceful resolution of
problems in personal, social and professional
relationships; help in creating a harmonious
environment for nurturing creativity and growth;
inspiration and help for nurses, doctors, hospice
workers, counselors, teachers, judges, public
servants and all who serve others.

• *World service:* ending of war, bringing of
peace, promoting of brotherhood and understanding, manifestation of divine justice in court-
rooms and between nations.

We are your companions, your brothers, your sisters, your servants.... We are sent to do a job for you.... Only call to us in the name of God, I AM THAT I AM, in the name of his Son Jesus Christ to enter your affairs.

Archangel Uriel

In 1985, Soviet cosmonauts reported seeing seven large angels with wings as big as jumbo jets from the window of the *Salyut 7* space station. "They were smiling," said one woman cosmonaut, "as though they shared in a glorious secret."

These angels bring to mind Archangel Uriel and the angels of peace. They are so large and powerful that they can simply dissolve seemingly insurmountable problems—even on a global scale—with the light of their beneficent smiles.

Uriel is not named in the Bible, but he is mentioned in other Jewish and Christian texts. In Jewish tradition, Archangel Uriel is called the "one who brings light to Israel." He is also known as an angel of judgment, thunder and earthquake. In the Fourth Book of Ezra, Uriel instructs Ezra in the secrets of the universe.

You can think of Uriel and the angels of peace as gigantic beings, like the ones seen by the cosmonauts. They can bring peace to troubled parts of the world, to your own home and even to a troubled mind or spirit. They work quickly and with great power. When you set them to work, you may see your problems disappear as swiftly as clouds after rain. When you ask them to tackle global problems, millions of angels go to work.

In the home, family and psyche, they work with the precision of microsurgeons. They will soothe disagreements and help you to remove the sources of agitation between family members. They will also help you get to the bottom of disquiet in your own soul by giving you the strength to let go of old hurts and overcome anger, irritation, self-defeating behavior, feelings of helplessness, and conscious and subconscious fear. See what a difference they can make when you invite them into your life!

—FIAT—

ARCHANGEL URIEL, MAKE ME AN
INSTRUMENT OF GOD'S PEACE!

ARCHANGEL URIEL'S EXERCISE FOR LETTING GO

Sit with your legs uncrossed and your feet flat on the floor in front of you. Focus your attention on your heart. Place your hands one on top of the other over your heart and then release them. Next put your hands on your knees, palms up. Relax and breathe gently.

Say tenderly to your soul and body, "Peace, be still." Repeat it as many times as you like, in multiples of three, while seeing yourself surrounded by the purple-gold-ruby light of the angels of peace.

Take a deep breath. As you breathe out, release your worries and concerns into the light. Watch as they dissolve on contact. Now inhale, seeing the light rush in to replace the burdens you have let go. Repeat three times.

Give the "Prayer of Saint Francis" (p. 106). Then say three times:

Archangel Uriel and angels of peace,
I accept the gift of peace in my heart,
in my soul, in my spirit,
in my body, in my mind!
Make me an instrument of God's peace!

ANGELS OF JOY

COLOR: Violet

ARCHANGEL: Zadkiel, "Righteousness of God"

SPIRITUAL HOME: Cuba

ASK THEM FOR:

- *Spiritual gifts:* soul freedom, happiness, joy, forgiveness, justice, mercy, dissolution of painful memories and negative traits.
- *Practical assistance:* tolerance; diplomacy; inspiration for scientists, engineers, architects, actors and performers.
- *World service:* dissolution of memories of strife between nations and ethnic groups; inspiration for the creative negotiation and writing of laws, regulations, fiscal and economic policies, trade and peace agreements.

—FIAT—

I AM THE LIVING FLAME OF COSMIC FREEDOM!

*N*egative memories can be one of the most difficult things to overcome. They affect the way we relate to other people and the way we think about ourselves. These memories don't even have to be in our conscious mind in order to hinder us. They may be below the surface but subtly influencing our relationships and how we approach problems and goals.

Zadkiel and the angels of joy can help you with these memories. In Jewish tradition, Zadkiel is known as the angel of benevolence, mercy and memory. He and his angels can teach you to use the violet flame, the flame of God that vibrates at the highest frequency, to dissolve memories that stop you from realizing your maximum potential.

The violet flame brings you soul freedom,

joy and fulfillment by liberating you from your own limiting behavior. It can help you to overcome your karma and the habit patterns that cause you to be vulnerable to pain, suffering, accidents and everything that puts you in need of the angels' help.

How does it work? In the past, all of us have misused God's energy by tying it up in negative thoughts and feelings. This energy weighs us down and keeps us from oneness with God. By invoking the violet flame through decrees, you can change this negative energy into positive energy. This is called transmutation. As Zadkiel has said, "All of this imprisoned energy must find freedom by the power of the violet flame!" Each time you give violet-flame decrees and transmute negative energy, you are liberated to receive more gifts and blessings from the angels.

Tell us how you liked this book!

Book title: _____

Comments: _____
_____

SUMMIT UNIVERSITY PRESS®

Non-Profit Publisher since 1975

What did you like the most? _____

How did you find this book? _____

☐ **YES! Send me FREE BOOK CATALOG**   ☐ I'm interested in more information

Name _____

Address _____

City _____ State _____ Zip Code _____

E-mail: _____ Phone no. _____

Your tax-deductible contributions make these publications available to the world.

Please make your checks payable to: Summit University Press, PO Box 5000, Gardiner, MT 59030.
Call us toll free at 1-800-245-5445. Outside the U.S.A., call 406-848-9500.
E-mail: tslinfo@tsl.org   www.summituniversitypress.com

491-HWA #4445 2/04

BUSINESS REPLY MAIL
FIRST-CLASS MAIL   PERMIT NO. 20   GARDINER MT

POSTAGE WILL BE PAID BY ADDRESSEE

SUMMIT UNIVERSITY ✦ PRESS

PO Box 5000

Gardiner, MT 59030-9900

The violet flame can also help to purify your physical body of the residue of drugs, pesticides and other chemicals that may be impairing your body's functions. To find out how Archangel Zadkiel and the angels of joy can fill you with joy, try the violet-flame decrees and visualizations on pages 108–11.

The greatest step to personal progress that you can take is the consistent use of the violet transmuting flame.

Archangel Zadkiel

DECREES AND PRAYERS TO THE ANGELS

Give the following preamble as you begin each session of devotions to the angels.

Preamble:

In the name of the I AM THAT I AM, I call to the seven archangels and their legions of light, I call to beloved Archangel _____ and the angels of _____.
I ask you to_____

_____ .

I ask that my call be multiplied and used for the assistance of all souls on this planet who are in need.

I thank you and I accept it done this hour in full power, according to the will of God.

TRAVELING PROTECTION

Visualization:

See Archangel Michael's presence in front of you, behind you, to the right and left, above and beneath you. Imagine yourself wearing a helmet and armour of blue steel that will prevent any physical or spiritual danger from reaching your body or mind. Hold this mental image throughout the day.

You can use this visualization to help others. When you are driving your car to work, see Archangel Michael's presence around every car on the highway and call for him to protect every car on every road in the entire world as well as anyone who is using any other form of transportation. Thus your call can be maximized and it can set millions of angels to work.

Start out by saying this slowly and deliberately. As you learn the decree, you can increase your speed.

Lord Michael before!
Lord Michael behind!
Lord Michael to the right!
Lord Michael to the left!
Lord Michael above!
Lord Michael below!
Lord Michael, Lord Michael wherever I go!

I AM his love protecting here!
I AM his love protecting here!
I AM his love protecting here!

MEDITATION
FOR ILLUMINATION

Visualization:

See your head surrounded by and infused with God's golden-yellow light. Next, see the angels of illumination flooding your whole body and the area around you, up to three feet in diameter, with this light. Feel yourself drawing in creativity and inspiration with every breath. See darkness, density and discouragement dissolved by the light.

O flame of Light bright and gold,
O flame most wondrous to behold,
I AM in every brain cell shining,
I AM Light's wisdom all divining.
Ceaseless, flowing fount of Illumination flaming,
I AM, I AM, I AM Illumination.

PRAYERS TO
THE ANGELS OF LOVE

Visualization:

Place your hands over your heart as you give these prayers to the angels of love. While you pour out devotion to God, see yourself one with all of life, one with the whole cosmic ocean of God's consciousness. Each time you say the words, visualize what they describe. These prayers will sustain your tie to Archangel Chamuel and the angels of love.

A ROSE UNFOLDING FAIR

As a rose unfolding fair
Wafts her fragrance on the air,
I pour forth to God devotion,
One now with the Cosmic Ocean.

THE BALM OF GILEAD

O Love of God, immortal Love,
Enfold all in thy ray;
Send compassion from above
To raise them all today!
In the fullness of thy power,
Shed thy glorious beams
Upon the earth and all thereon
Where life in shadow seems.
Let the Light of God blaze forth
To cut men free from pain;
Raise them up and clothe them, God,
With thy mighty I AM name!

AFFIRMATIONS
FOR ANGELIC GUIDANCE

Visualization:

As you give these affirmations, see Gabriel and the angels of guidance pouring into your body, mind and soul a white light that infuses you with confidence, joy and direction. Surrender to God's plan for you and rest secure in the knowledge that you will be shown how to fulfill it. Remember, whenever you say "I AM...," you are saying "God in me is...."

I AM the pure, radiant God-design
  of my own being
I AM bringing to the world the fullness
  of the mission that is my own
I AM one in the heart of God
I AM the Love of God
I AM the Love of heaven
I AM the Love of the angels
I AM the Love of the archangels
I AM the Love that is real
I AM the coming into fruition of the great
  purpose for which I first drew breath

AFFIRMATIONS
FOR CHRIST WHOLENESS

Instructions:

Give these affirmations for the healing of yourself and anyone who needs healing of body, mind, soul or spirit. Begin with a prayer to Raphael and the angels of healing, stating the name and condition of the person in need.

Visualization:

After you have given this decree for awhile, you will have it memorized and you will be able to say it with your eyes closed. When your eyes are closed, you can better visualize white and green healing light enveloping the ailing person and the diseased or injured organs. See the angels directing light into the area of the body that is in need of healing. Then see the entire body infused with intense white and green light and each cell becoming whole. Visualize the body liberated from the condition.

I AM God's perfection manifest
   In body, mind and soul—
I AM God's direction flowing
   To heal and keep me whole!

O atoms, cells, electrons
   Within this form of mine,
Let heaven's own perfection
   Make me now divine!

The spirals of Christ wholeness
   Enfold me by his might—
I AM the Master Presence
   Commanding, "Be all Light!"

AFFIRMATIONS
TO THE ANGELS OF PEACE

Instructions:

Give these affirmations whenever you are concerned about the outcome of a project you are working on or about strife in your family, community or nation. Trust in the angels of peace to provide the perfect resolution.

Visualization:

See the beautiful purple, gold and ruby energy of Uriel and the angels of peace surrounding and enfolding the people or situation that you are concerned about. See how the negative energy is dissolved by the power of peace.

I AM the gentle rain of peace
I AM the manifestation of divine
    perfectionment
I AM the great heartbeat of divine love
    from on high

I AM the power of infinite love and
    compassion within

I AM the flame of love that will sustain all

I AM the realization of the power of love

I AM the externalization of the quality
    of divine freedom

I AM the quality of infinite peace in
    manifestation

I AM the power of tranquility

I AM the power of great tides of love
    and peace bringing to an end the
    contamination of discord and despair

I AM the renewal of hope in hearts that
    have no hope

I AM understanding wherever there are
    ears to hear and hearts to embrace

I AM the freedom of men from the
    shackles of war

I AM a messenger of peace

THE PRAYER OF
SAINT FRANCIS OF ASSISI

Instructions:

Use in your daily meditations and with Archangel Uriel's Exercise for Letting Go (p. 84).

Lord,
Make me an instrument of thy peace.
Where there is hatred let me sow love;
Where there is injury, pardon;
Where there is doubt, faith;
Where there is despair, hope;
Where there is darkness, light; and
Where there is sadness, joy.

O Divine Master,
Grant that I may not so much
Seek to be consoled as to console;

To be understood as to understand;
To be loved as to love.
For it is in giving that we receive,
It is in pardoning that we are pardoned, and
It is in dying that we are born to eternal
    life.

AFFIRMATIONS
TO THE ANGELS OF JOY

Visualization:

The violet flame ranges in color from a pale lilac to a brilliant amethyst. Whenever you decree to Zadkiel and the angels of joy, see this flame as a giant bonfire that surrounds you. Watch the angels take from you all of your burdens, worries and concerns and throw them into the flame, where they are transformed into positive energy.

I AM the boundlessness of the Spirit of Light
I AM the awareness of the glory of God
I AM the awareness of the power of God
I AM awareness of the violet flame,
    which is able by the power of God to
    transmute all shadowed substance into
    the purity of the great Cosmic Light

I AM the blessed feeling of God-happiness
  through the very pores of my skin
  and the pores of my mind and the
  pores of my heart
I AM freedom from limitation
I AM freedom from fear
I AM freedom from worry and overconcern
I AM the commitment of my soul and
  total being into the hands of the
  infinite God
I AM God-freedom in manifestation
I AM God-happiness in manifestation
I accept my freedom now!

I AM THE VIOLET FLAME

Instruction:

Direct the energy of the violet flame into all internal and external obstacles keeping you from happiness and freedom in God.

Visualization:

See Zadkiel and the angels of joy directing the violet flame into every cell and atom of your being and into the situation that you are praying about. You can imagine the violet flame working just like a giant chalkboard eraser, wiping out all pain, despair, suffering and limitation.

I AM the violet flame
    In action in me now
I AM the violet flame
    To Light alone I bow
I AM the violet flame
    In mighty cosmic power
I AM the Light of God
    Shining every hour
I AM the violet flame
    Blazing like a sun
I AM God's sacred power
    Freeing every one

PICTURE CREDITS: **Cover:** *Tobias and the Angel,* Giovanni Girolamo Savoldo, Scala/Art Resource, N.Y.; **Page 20:** *Court of Angels,* detail, reprinted by permission of The British Library, 7894; **54:** Appears on the facade of the Stanford Memorial Church, Stanford University, Calif., used with permission; **86:** *The Dream of Saint Joachim,* detail, Giotto di Bondone, Alinari/Art Resource, N.Y.; **88** and **92:** *The Attainment of the Holy Grail,* detail, Edward Burne-Jones, reprinted by permission of Birmingham Museums and Art Gallery.

FOR INFORMATION: If you would like a free catalog of books, tapes and CDs or information about seminars and workshops featuring the spiritual techniques discussed in this book, contact Summit University Press, PO Box 5000, Corwin Springs, MT 59030-5000 USA.
Tel: 1-800-245-5445 (or 406-848-9500)
Fax: 1-800-221-8307 (or 406-848-9555)
E-mail us at info@summituniversitypress.com
www.summituniversitypress.com

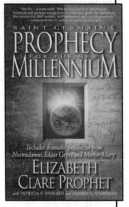